LOVE NOTES

Love Notes from the Father

BRITT FAIR

WESTBOW
PRESS®
A DIVISION OF THOMAS NELSON
& ZONDERVAN

WestBow Press books may be ordered through booksellers or by contacting:

WestBow Press
A Division of Thomas Nelson & Zondervan
1663 Liberty Drive
Bloomington, IN 47403
www.westbowpress.com
844-714-3454

Interior Image Credit: Britt Fair

ISBN: 978-1-6642-4782-6 (sc)
ISBN: 978-1-6642-4783-3 (hc)
ISBN: 978-1-6642-4781-9 (e)

Library of Congress Control Number: 2021921404

Print information available on the last page.

WestBow Press rev. date: 10/20/2021

ACKNOWLEDGMENTS

My heart overflows with humility and gratitude to all those who helped make this book possible. You would think someone who wrote a book could find the words to express how truly thankful I am, but every word just seems to falls short. The amount of encouragement, love, support, and sheer excitement I have received from the people in my life that I shared this process with has been incredible, so from the bottom of my heart, I thank you.

To my husband, Nate, your first reaction when I told you what G-D spoke to me, and the hope and faith in this you've displayed along the way, has touched my heart tremendously. It has been my strongest arm of encouragement to have your support and to see your faith shine so brightly.

To my mom, Toni, thank you for making it your highest priority in our lives to teach us that our relationship with G-D is the most important thing in life. Thank you for always praying for us through everything. Your laying of that foundation taught me where my treasures and riches truly are.

To Pastor Jessica and Pastor Donny, thank you both for all that you do, for all of your prayers and the life you have spoken into me, into my husband, and into our family. Thank you for planting those seeds of life, encouragement, and increase; thank you for sewing your time into us and into our children. Thank you for being so strong in your faith and relationships with G-D in such a way that it inspires and excites us to learn more and desire a closer, more intimate relationship with our Father.

To my dear friends who have helped make me the person I am today, who have loved me and encouraged me in the ways I should go, pushed me to do good, spoken words of life, wisdom, and anointing into me, my marriage, my children, my family; I thank you. And I honor each one of you. I pray and declare harvests returned to you in double and triple portions of all the good seeds you have sewn into the kingdom of heaven.

INTRODUCTION

One of the things that I love about G-D is the way He talks to us. He created us so unique it's only fitting that He would talk to us in ways just as unique as His creation. He's so personal and He loves to talk to us! And why wouldn't He? There's *so* much He has to tell us!

He used a fiery bush to get Moses's attention and speak to him (Exodus 3:1–15). Samuel, He woke up three times audibly calling his name (1 Samuel, chapter 3). He sent an angel to speak to Mary about being chosen to be the mother of J-SUS (Luke 1:26–38), and He used a dream to speak to Joseph concerning Mary being pregnant (Matthew 1:18–25). He even used a donkey to speak to Balaam (Numbers 22:21–39).

G-D often speaks to me in dreams, and He also shows me things in my spirit. Most of the time He will tell me about what He has shown me, give a word for it or for the person that it's for. Then there are times when there is not an immediate explanation, and I'll have to sit and pray on it for a little while, or I'll discuss it with a couple of trusted friends who are mature in their walks with G-D. What I also do when G-D shows me things, is draw out the pictures that He gives me, and I'll write down the word with it that He spoke to my heart. If you're not already familiar with this, it's called Prophetic Art.

Prophetic Art is art that helps to show the heart of our Father. I'm sure you hear people say all the time that they're *visual* learners where they have to see things to help themselves understand, or they're *tactile* learners where they need to touch things and work with their hands on something in order for things to "click". Prophetic art is a way to put a visual to the words of encouragement, or words of knowledge, that are given. Someone can be told something over and over and over again and still need it explained "one more time", but once you *show* them, they've got it! They'll never need it explained again because now that they've seen it, it's been ingrained into their hearts and minds and they won't be forgetting it anytime soon!

In Hebrews 10:24–25 (NIV), it says:

> *And let us consider how we may spur one another on toward love and good deeds, not giving up meeting together, as some are in the habit of doing, but encouraging one another – and all the more as you see the Day approaching.*

In 1 Thessalonians 5:11 (ESV) it says,

> *Therefore encourage one another and build one another up, just as you are doing.*

And again in Philemon 1:7 (NIV),

> *"Your love has given me great joy and encouragement, because you, brother, have refreshed the hearts of the L-RD's people."*

There are several other verses in the Bible that talk about encouraging others in one way or another. Why is that? Why does that matter if we are encouraging others or not? Because our adversary the devil walks about like a roaring lion, seeking whom he may devour (1 Peter 5:8), and even the strongest of the strongest can grow weary and get discouraged. There is not one person who has ever lived, or ever will, that can say they went through life without a time where they felt fear or despair, or worn down from certain things they were facing. Even J-SUS, our Savior, the Son of G-D, had His moment in the garden of Gethsemane where His soul was so "deeply grieved, to the point of death" (Matthew 26:38), because He knew the extent He was about to have to suffer. He asked His closest friends to come with Him because He wanted, needed, them there. He even asked G-D if there was *any* other way for things to be done than the way they were about to happen; but He was so good to say still, "Not as I will, but as You will" (Matthew 26:39).

Even when you're going through things that you feel like no one else could possibly understand, *know* that G-D sees you, and He understands completely. It was for moments like yours, people in situations of despair like yours, for people like you; it was for *you,* that G-D told us to encourage each other. Because He knew we would face these times where we needed hope, where we needed encouragement, where we needed truth and life spoken over us and into us. Because He knew *you* would need it. And that is exactly what this is; a book filled with prophetic images that G-D has shown me over a span of years, and the words that He gave along with them.

Now that we've established *what* this is, I'd like to talk about the events that came about as to *why* this is. As I stated, some of these sketches are several years old, so why am I just now sharing them like this? Honestly, it's because I had never in my wildest dreams thought to do anything like this before. I have always loved art and drawing; I even started a small art business doing commissioned work years ago and I love it immensely. I have also always loved literature, reading, as well as writing and have always had something in the works of fiction or autobiographical as far back as I can remember. It just *never* occurred to me to combine the two! Fast forward through my life a couple decades, and skip over the testimony part for now (that's for another time), and we get to where I was working in a place that I very much enjoyed. It was a huge blessing to my family and me in a time of need, and it felt like somewhere I could settle down and grow in for the foreseeable future. While I was there, a gallstone I'd had for a couple years was becoming increasingly painful. For those two years I had done what I could to manage it without surgery (in my opinion pretty successfully) but we had finally reached the point where it needed to come out. Skip ahead a bit, I had the surgery, my job was great about it, and I was recovering. Pretty immediately upon returning to work, though, things began to feel off and very unsettled, and I couldn't figure out why. It didn't take long before G-D started to tell me that I was not supposed to be there anymore. This was surprising news to me, as my plans were to be there for the foreseeable future.

That's always the thing about G-D, though, isn't it? Our plans for ourselves are never quite what He has in mind. That makes me laugh a lot of the time because I always feel like I should have seen it coming. So, as

I was trying to convince G-D of all the reasons I was supposed to stay in that job, He was steadily telling me no, and that He had something for me that was better; somewhere that I could be close to my children. I finally said 'Yes, L-RD', and told Him that I would start looking for a new job, and when I found something I would put in my two week's notice. Ready for another one of those, *"You didn't see that coming?"* moments? Once I told G-D "Okay, yes, but here's how *I'm* going to do it," He then told me that I could not end that current month still employed there. Want to know where in the month we were when He told me that? Smack dab in the middle, of course. That meant that I had to give my two week's notice *right* then. And let me tell you, that was *not* an easy thing to do for an introvert! It also didn't give me much time to talk to my husband about it, either. "Hey, honey, I know I don't have another job lined up or anything that even looks promising right now, but G-D told me to put in my two week's anyway, so I did…" My husband was understandably confused and a little thrown back by that at first, but only at first. He knows my prayer life and knew that I was acting in obedience to G-D.

As the days continued, it seemed more and more strained at work. I was putting in applications left and right, several every day. Since I had no idea what G-D had in store for me, I was applying for all kinds of things. Pretty much anything that popped up that would have favorable hours to manage work and family, and that was closer to home. There's one more week to go in my two week's notice, and I'm driving home from work, just talking to G-D. It's a fifteen minute drive, so we had a little time. I was telling Him how much I just wanted what He had for me, and that I wanted to be in *His* will for my life, not my own, so I was trusting Him. But I also didn't know exactly what He had for me, so that began to be my heart's cry to Him. Not angry, not sad, not desperate, just sincere.

"G-D, what do *You* want me to do?"

Now, we're going to pause here briefly; I've already told you that a lot of these sketches are from years ago. And that is an entirely other conversation that I've had with G-D on *many* occasions.

When I would do prophetic art in church, it was done quickly during worship. I would draw with it in my lap, eventually I was given a table, and then another pastor even set up an art table to draw with the worship team. Occasionally, G-D would give me something to draw for specific people and give it to them, but the majority of the time it was for everyone, to encourage the body of Chr-st. So through the years I filled up several art books. I would have them ready after services to show everyone, and then I'd close the book and put it aside. The more books that filled up and were put in a drawer at home, the more that bothered me. It didn't bother me because it was something I wanted to show off, on the contrary, a lot of times I was embarrassed at how messy the sketches were because the lighting was so dark during worship it was often hard to see, and I was sketching so quickly because of time. So these were not my "show-stopping" best works. It was very humbling to have people see them when I saw so much technically wrong with them. No, what bothered me was that I knew that G-D had shown me each and every one of those drawings for a purpose, *His* purpose, and they were just hidden away in a drawer. How were they helping or encouraging anyone like that? How was I using G-D's gift that He *trusted* me with, when I couldn't figure out how to get out and reach people with them? I didn't even know who all those people were that needed them, because who really knows what's going on in other peoples' lives unless you're close to them and they confide in you? Even then, some of the people we're closest to we have no idea what they're truly battling with behind closed doors. I can't tell you how many times I was surprised by certain peoples' reactions to the art, and even more surprised by why it touched them so deeply when they opened up and told me about what they were going through. Because I just didn't know. And how could I have known? But G-D knew.

Now, back to the drive home from work that last week; I hadn't been talking to G-D about prophetic art, or even about regular art. It was honestly the furthest thing from my mind. All that I had wanted to know that day, in that moment, was *what* G-D wanted me to do? Because whatever that was, *that's* what I wanted to do. And in my sincerity, He was so good to answer. He said, in that voice that's so gentle but so strong, that still, small voice that's so soft it always surprises me just how clear and resonating it really is:

"I want you to put the prophetic art into a book."

Let me tell you… my mind was blown when He said that. It was so obvious I could not believe that all these years something like that had never even crossed my mind! Then He told me it was going to be called "Love Notes" and I lost it. I mean, how I could expect anything less than something so profoundly simple I don't even know. G-D just knows what He's doing!

When we can just stop, get out of the way, and let Him move, He will literally leave you speechless. And His timing is so perfect, too. He knows just who needs what, and *when* they need it. So when I tell you that G-D was thinking of *you* when He told me to write this book, He *was*! He has something for you, something that He knew you would need in your own life, or maybe even something that He wants to use you to share with someone else going through a difficult time, and their hearts are crying out because they are weary. They've battled and battled and it feels like the blows just keep on coming, and they just need something to give them a little hope. Something they can cling to; something that gives them encouragement and feeds their strength to get up and continue to fight the good fight. Because all is *not* lost! G-D hears them. G-D hears *you*! He sees you. And He so deeply and passionately loves you with all of His heart. He wants you to know that today. He wants you to *see* that today. So as you turn through these pages, read them knowing that these love notes were written from a heart that fervently beats for *you*.

CHAPTER 1

I'm sure you've already noticed that the name of G-D is not spelled out. You will continue to see if that way, and any other name referring to Him or J-SUS, throughout this book. The reason is simply that I had a personal conviction a few years ago about the name of the L-RD. It is holy and powerful; there is authority in His name (Matt. 28:18; Psalm 148:13;Acts 4:12; Phil. 2:9; etc.). One of the commandments evens says, "You shall not take the name of the L-RD your G-D in vain," (Exodus 20:7 – NKJV). Because His name *is* so holy, I don't want that authority and the holiness of His name to become common to me in my life, so, when writing, it causes me to take a little extra time and not just rush through it. It gives me reason to pause and reflect on why I'm taking that extra time for His name. It's not just any name, and I want to honor Him in every way that I can, because He *is* worthy.

In the Hebrew written language, (minus a couple of exceptions) vowels are not used, so the name of J-SUS, J-HOVAH, is spelled YHVH. There are a few reasons why Jewish culture does this. I'm not going to delve into all of those reasons, as that's not what this book is about, but I greatly encourage taking a deeper look into them. One of the main reasons is to show honor and respect to the mighty, holy name of our Father and Redeemer. For the sake of simply avoiding confusion for readers unfamiliar with this, I only mark out the first vowel. I would like to reiterate that this is something I personally felt led to do to honor G-D, and to always remember the importance and power of His name.

In a time where it seems like we're seeing more hatred, division, and chaos in the world than ever before, it's easy to get so caught up in the negative that's going on around us that we forget to bring something positive into the mix. I feel like that's one of the reasons this is such an important time for this book. It's meant to be an encouragement to everyone who opens its pages. Whether they're looking for encouragement or not, whether they're in a good place in their lives or a difficult one, or just somewhere in between, I believe that there is something on at least one of these pages that will touch your heart and open the doors to let G-D's love come in and shine; to show you how much love He really does have for *you*.

As you go throughout your days at work, at home, or just out and about, remember to be a light in this dark world. There is a saying that you may or may not have heard before; "you may be the only J-SUS someone sees today." So what kind of J-SUS are you showing them? Are you representing Him well?

"Be kind to one another, tenderhearted, forgiving one another, as G-D in CHR-ST forgave you." (Ephesians 4:32 ESV)

"Put on then, as G-D's chosen ones, holy and beloved, compassionate hearts, kindness, humility, meekness, and patience, bearing with one another and, if one has a complaint against another, forgiving each other; as the L-RD has forgiven you, so you also must forgive." (Colossians 3:12–13 ESV)

CHAPTER 2

Therefore I tell you, do not be anxious about your life, what you will eat or what you will drink, nor about your body, what you will put on. Is not life more than food, and the body more than clothing? Look at the birds of the air: they neither sow nor reap nor gather into barns, and yet your heavenly Father feeds them. Are you not of more value than they? And which of you by being anxious can add a single hour to his span of life? (Matthew 6:25–27 ESV)

G-D tells us to "fear not" 365 times in the Bible. A definition of fear is: "a feeling of anxiety concerning the outcome of something or the safety and well-being of someone."

Why are we told that so many times? Because every day we are in the palm of *His* hands. He is with us, He is for us, He is there to pick us up when we are weak, and He is there to provide for us when we are in need. We are not called to be fearful; we are called to be *faithful*.

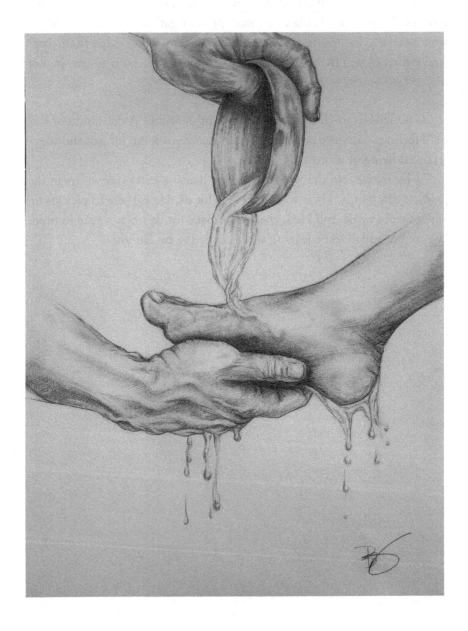

Husbands, love your wives, just as Chr-st also loved the church and gave Himself for her, that He might sanctify and cleanse her with the washing with water by the word, that He might present her to himself as a glorious church, not having spot or wrinkle or any such thing, but that she should be holy and without blemish. So husbands ought to love their own wives as their own bodies; he who loves his wife loves himself. For no one ever hated his own flesh, but nourishes and cherishes it, just as the L-RD does the church. (Ephesians 5:25–29 – NKJV)

The original of this drawing was given as a wedding gift to some friends. I prayed on what to do for them, and this is what I was shown.

Marriage is a beautiful covenant before G-D between husband and wife. It is a sacred thing to be honored, treasured, and respected, forsaking all others. It's also a humbling thing, as we are to put our spouse before ourselves. And what better example of humility, honor, and love, than the washing of feet. Before J-SUS went to die, He washed the feet of His disciples. He, the Perfect One, the True King, willingly and humbly served those He loved.

I HAVE SUPPLIED.
I WILL CONTINUE TO
PROVIDE FOR YOU.

"I have supplied. I will continue to provide for you," says the L-RD.

Isaac spoke up and said to his father Abraham, "Father?" "Yes, my son?" Abraham replied. "The fire and wood are here," Isaac said, "but where is the lamb for the burnt offering?" Abraham answered, "G-D Himself will provide the lamb for the burnt offering, my son." And the two of them went on together. (Genesis 22:7–8 – NIV)

Abraham looked up and there in a thicket he saw a ram caught by its horns. He went over and took the ram and sacrificed it as a burnt offering instead of his son. So Abraham called that place The L-RD Will Provide. And to this day it is said, "On the mountain of the L-RD it will be provided." (Genesis 22:13–14 – NIV)

When G-D says He will provide, He means it. There is no place that G-D will take you where a way is not made. Whatever He is calling you to do, wherever He is calling you to do it, even if it doesn't make sense and maybe even seems a little scary, when you are called, the way has *already* been made for you. Trust in the L-RD, truly seek His face and His plans for you, let Him guide your steps, and know that He is faithful in His promises.

You are called *royalty*! You are sons and daughters of the One True King! The Great I AM! The Alpha and Omega. The Beginning and the End! Yahweh, Jehovah, Messiah, and Yeshua! It's time to pick up that sword, dust off that crown, and start acting like it!

"My sons and daughters, *remember who you are*! You do not have to grovel for breadcrumbs, nor do you have to beg for any need. I have prepared a seat for you at My table. I have placed My signet ring on your hand and given you the authority!" – G-D

Then the seventy returned with joy, saying, "L-RD, even the demons are subject to us in Your Name." And He said to them, "I saw Satan fall like lightning from heaven. Behold, I give you the authority to trample on serpents and scorpions, and over all the power of the enemy, and nothing shall by any means hurt you. Nevertheless do not rejoice in this, that the spirits are subject to you, but rather rejoice because your names are written in heaven." (Luke 10:17–20 NKJV)

No longer can the enemy stifle your words. G-D *spoke* things into existence, so you need to un-bind your mouth, and *shout* the truth of G-D! Prophesy and *speak*!

"*Speak*, sons and daughters! Open your mouths and let My Holy Spirit pour forth through you! Not your words, but Mine. I have created you as living vessels. Open your mouths and let Me shake the nations." – G-D

Then one of the seraphim flew to me, having in his hand a live coal which he had taken with the tongs from the altar. And he touched my mouth with it, and said: "Behold, this has touched your lips; Your iniquity is taken away, And your sin purged." Also I heard the voice of the L-RD, saying: "Whom shall I send, And who will go for Us?" Then I said, "Here am I! Send me!" (Isaiah 6:6–8 – NKJV)

"G-D playing with the box that you tried to put Him in"

We oftentimes put our own limitations on G-D when He is telling us that there is something so much bigger that He has in store for us. What we *think* we need and want, most of the time, if not all the time, G-D has something even greater in store for us. We have to learn to trust Him with our all, and stop getting in His way as He works on us. The limits that we have, He does not. And if we allow Him to have His way in us, He is faithful to show us just how great He is as He breaks through the ceiling and tears down every wall of false limitations in your life. Get into that intimate place with G-D, and seek His face. He has so much He wants to show you, and so much He wants to do through you!

But J-SUS looked at them and said, "With man this is impossible, but with G-D all things are possible." (Matthew 19:26 – ESV)

Great is our L-RD, and abundant in power; His understanding is beyond measure. (Psalm 147:5 – ESV)

1 Samuel 9:21

And Saul answered and said "Am I not a Benjamite, of the smallest of the tribes of Israel? and my family the least of all the families of the tribe of Benjamin? wherefore then speakest thou so to me?

(upon Samuel telling him God had appointed him to be King.

You are not too small too be used by God, you are not too young to be used by God, the family you come from is not too unimportant for you to be used by God, God makes you bigger then you are if you let Him reside in and create big things with you.

And Saul answered and said, "Am I not a Benjamite, of the smallest of the tribes of Israel? And my family the least of all the families of the tribe of Benjamin? Wherefore then speakest though so to me?" (1 Samuel 9:21– KJV)

— *(upon Samuel telling him G-D had appointed him to be king.)*

You are not too small to be used by G-D. You are not too young to be used by G-D, and the family you come from is not too "unimportant" for you to be used by G-D. G-D makes you bigger than you are, and if you let Him reside in you, He will create big things with you!

G-D has a habit of taking what the world deems as insignificant, and using it to create the extraordinary! Don't ever let your circumstances, your insecurities, or what you feel you lack, put a limit on what G-D wants to do in your life.

The power of praise is evident in the storm. I will Praise You in the storm! For in my praise to You, Your presence resides with the power to calm the storm.

Therefore I will give thanks to You, L-RD, among the nations, and I will sing praises to Your Name. (2 Samuel 22:50 – NASV)

I call upon the L-RD, who is worthy to be praised, and I am saved from my enemies. (Psalm 18:3 – ESV)

What mightier name is there than the name of G-D? The Name above all names? Let Your Name be ever on my lips, Oh G-D, that my voice of praise to You would keep my heart, and my eyes, set like flint upon You, and not on the circumstances surrounding me. Though the waves may crash and the thunder may roar, I will not be moved, for my eyes are on You. My heart is set upon You, and my praise lays the foundation for You to build upon.

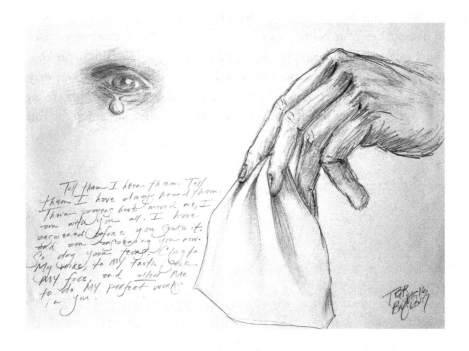

Tell them I hear them. Tell
them I have always heard them.
Their prayers have moved me, I
am with you all. I have
answered before you asked it,
and am answering you now.
So dry your tears. Cling to
My voice, to My Faith; seek
MY face, and allow Me
to do MY perfect works
in you.

"Tell them I hear them. Tell them I have *always* heard them. Their prayers have moved Me; I Am with you all. I have answered before you spoke it, and am answering you now. So dry your tears. Cling to My voice, to My truth; seek My face, and *allow* Me to do My perfect works in you."

– G-D

Then he said to me, "Don't be afraid, Daniel. Since the first day you began to pray for understanding and to humble yourself before your G-D, your request has been heard in heaven. I have come in answer to your prayer. (Daniel 10:12 – NLT)

"Before they call I will answer; while they are yet speaking I will hear." (Isaiah 65:24 – NIV)

Sometimes in the midst of hard times and struggles, it's easy to feel like our prayers are falling on deaf ears. We're praying and interceding, and still we feel like we're getting nothing.

Daniel fasted and prayed for three weeks to get his answer; he interceded with all he had and contended the heavens for his answer! So much so, that at the end of it he said there was no strength left in him. There was a spiritual battle going on that detained the angel from bringing Daniel his answer, but he told Daniel that G-D answered his prayers that very first day. When we feel like G-D is silent, or our prayers aren't being heard, *know* that they *are* heard! The answer has already been given! Don't give up. Don't let the waiting cause you to grow weary. Push through and contend the heavens, and trust that G-D has heard you and has already spoken!

The wicked run away when no one is chasing them, but the godly are as bold as lions. (Proverbs 28:1 – NLT)

In whom we have boldness and access with confidence through our faith in him. (Ephesians 3:12 – ESV)

When the world around us is saying one thing, we can stand strong and bold, unwavering and sure in who we are in Chr-st, and what He says about us. We are *His* sons, daughters, and heirs to the throne. We are called to walk in righteousness and sure footing in Him. We don't have to be afraid or intimidated or feel pressured when the world says to act a certain way we know is wrong.

Do you think a king trembles at the chastisement of his servants? Do you think he doubts his authority because of cruel words from people in his land? No! He *knows* who he was born to, he knows his birthright, and he will stand on that authority until the end of his days. So should we also *know* who we belong to, and remember the authority we have been given. Do not back down in the evil day, do not grow weary. Stand strong and as bold as lions!

Where The Spirit of the Lord is,
there is Freedom and Joy!
Jesus, God's Perfect Son,
Gave His life For you
to be able to experience
Freedom and Resurrection
power!

Where the Spirit of the L-RD is, there is freedom and joy! J-SUS, G-D's perfect Son, gave His life for you to be able to experience freedom and resurrection power!

Now the L-RD is the Spirit, and where the Spirit of the L-RD is, there is freedom. (2 Corinthians 3:17 – NIV)

"Rejoice in the L-RD always. I will say it again: Rejoice!" (Phillipians 4:4 – NIV)

"Rejoice always, pray continually, give thanks in all circumstances; for this is G-D's will for you in Chr-st J-sus." (1 Thessalonians 5:16–18 – NIV)

We are called to be joyful and rejoice in *all* circumstances, which is not always easy. It feels downright impossible sometimes. But G-D is the G-D of impossible things, and through the Holy Spirit, we can receive joy, unspeakable joy! We can have that Shalom peace that surpasses understanding if we let G-D touch our hearts in the midst of our circumstances. Then we can have a kind of joy that just doesn't make sense. When other people can't figure out why we're not falling apart and why we haven't thrown in the towel yet, when they're asking how in the world we have a smile on our face, we can testify that it's because of G-D who is in us, and that He is able to touch our spirit deeper than anything else can reach.

You are never "too far gone" for G-D. You may think that you have messed up one too many times and feel like G-D has just had enough of you; like you have no more chances at forgiveness. But you couldn't be further from the truth! G-D is still right by your side, ready to embrace you with open arms. Ready to wash you clean and heal your wounds, ready to forgive you. He's waiting, eager to hear that moment when you cry out to Him, "Yes, L-RD! I need You! I need Your strength to fill me again!" And He will rush to you to fill you with His unending love. Do not listen to the lie that you have done "too much" wrong. Just call on G-D, He is ready for you to come back to Him!

Therefore say to them, 'Thus says the L-RD of hosts: "Return to Me," says the L-RD of hosts, "and I will return to you," says the L-RD of hosts. – (Zechariah 1:3 – NKJV)

"If you return to the Almighty, you will be restored; If you remove unrighteousness far from your tent, (Job 22:23 – NASB 1995)

"May I have this dance?" – G-D

G-D desires that intimate worship with you. It's time to get up out of your seat, He is waiting for you on the dance floor.

Don't be shy; there's no need to be shy with the One who created you! He knows your every thought; He's numbered every strand on your head. He calls you His beloved, and loves you with the purest, truest, deepest love you could ever know.

Then David danced before the L-RD with all his might; (2 Samuel 6:14 – NKJV)

The L-RD your G-D is in your midst, the Mighty One, will save; He will rejoice over you with gladness; He will quiet you with His love; he will rejoice over you with singing. (Zephaniah 3:17 – NKJV)

I am Judas' kiss, but you love me anyway.
See now I am the man who yelled out from the crowd,
For your blood to be spilled on this earth shaking ground
… But you love my anyway

Those are just a few lines from the song *You Love Me Anyway* by Sidewalk Prophets. It's a beautiful song, but if you really listen to the lyrics you will hear such a deep truth. Judas was the one who betrayed J-sus. He signaled to the soldiers which one He was by kissing His cheek upon greeting Him.

Maybe you feel like you've sinned "too greatly" or just "too much" in general and there is no turning it around. You feel like there is no way you can be forgiven. Maybe you even feel like you have betrayed G-D with how you've been living your life and the things you have spoken. I'm telling you now, it's not too late. You haven't done "too much". Judas betrayed J-sus, sent Him to be brutally beaten and crucified, but J-sus *still* loved him. And He went to the cross willingly for each one of us, including Judas; including *you*. He didn't die for the "good" people, or the nice people, or just for His "favorites", He died for *all* of us. And you know what? You *are* His favorite, too. He loves you so much more than you can imagine. Don't forget that! Remind yourself of that every day, because every day, no matter what, it is true!

He redeems me from death and crowns me with love and tender mercies. (Psalm 103:4 – NLT)

IT'S TIME TO
TOSS OUT OUR
OLD, TIRED,
SENSES OF THE
FLESH. PUT
ON NEW EYES,
TO SEE THROUGH
GOD'S PERSPECTIVE,
NEW EARS TO HEAR
HIS VOICE, NEW
HEART THAT IS
SENSITIVE TO HIS
PRESENCE, NEW LIP
TO SPEAK HIS WORD
NEW FEET TO
PLANT FIRMLY ON HIS
PATH AND FOLLOW
WHERE HE LEADS,
NEW HANDS TO DO THE
FAITHFUL WORKS OF
A SERVANT.

It's time to toss out our old, tired, senses of the flesh and put on *new* eyes, to see through G-D's perspective. New ears to hear His voice, a new Heart that is sensitive to His presence, new lips to speak His Words; new feet to plant firmly on His path and follow where He leads, new hands to do the faithful works of a servant.

Therefore, if anyone is in CHR-ST, he is a new creation; old things have passed away; behold, all things have become new! (2 Corinthians 5:17 – NKJV)

A *new* creation! Do you know what that really means? It means that you no longer have to feel the weight of the past. It's not going into tomorrow with you! Let it go, and move forward with G-D. Take those next steps that bring you closer to Him, deeper into His presence, and further *away* from the person you used to be, because no matter how many times the world will try to remind you of that old person, that's *not* who you are anymore. Don't look behind you again. Throw away that rearview mirror and set your eyes on what is in front of you!

He just wants you to come. Come and sit at His feet and soak in His presence. He has so much He wants to tell you, so much He wants to pour out into you. So much love to give. Just come.

And she had a sister called Mary, who also sat at J-sus' feet and heard His word. But Martha was distracted with much serving, and she approached Him and said, "L-rd, do You not care that my sister has left me to serve alone? Therefore tell her to help me." And J-sus answered and said to her, "Martha, Martha, you are worried and troubled about many things. But one thing is needed, and Mary has chosen that good part, which will not be taken away from her." (Luke 10:39–42 – NKJV)

It's *so* easy to get caught up with life and the craziness of everything we have on our plates. How many times have we heard someone say - or said ourselves - "There just isn't enough time in the day!" Truer words were never spoken! Between busy schedules, work, activities, chores, and necessities, as well as trying to just find a minute to breathe in between, it can get so hard to even make sure you're getting enough sleep at night. But we have to *make* time to get alone with G-D. Like J-sus said, that is choosing the good part, the *one thing* that is *needed*. We *need* G-D. We need that intimacy and refreshing with Him otherwise we will wear ourselves out and get to the point where we just don't even feel like it. When we make that time for Him, He restores our soul. It doesn't make all those things we have to do disappear or magically get done without us, but it *does* make our attitudes better while we're doing them. When we're refreshed with G-D, we can have a peace and joy while we go throughout our day. We can be sensitive to His quickening when we come across someone He wants us to minister to. When we're wrapped up in His love and carry that time of intimacy with Him throughout our day, it is easier for us to *respond* in that Holy Spirit atmosphere, rather than *react* from a place of fleshly emotion.

Because Martha chose not to prioritize her time with J-sus, resulting in her not spending any time with Him at all, she was steadily growing bitter in her flesh as the day went on. Mary, however, chose to soak in the presence of the Messiah.

Come close to G-D, and G-D will come close to you. Wash your hands, you sinners; purify your hearts, for your loyalty is divided between G-D and the world. (James 4:8 – NLT)

You keep him in perfect peace whose mind is stayed on you, because he trusts in you. (Isaiah 26:3 – ESV)

But above all pursue His kingdom and righteousness, and all these things will be given to you as well. (Matthew 6:33 – NET)

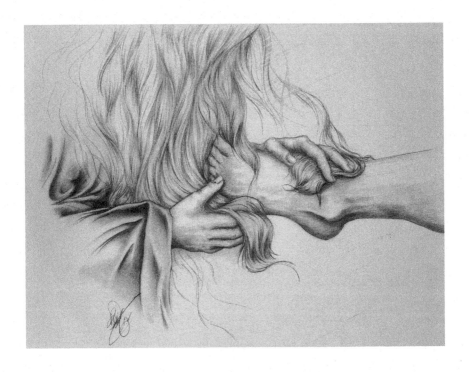

Then Mary took a pound of a very costly oil of spikenard, anointed the feet of J-SUS, and wiped His feet with her hair. And the house was filled with the fragrance of the oil. But one of His disciples, Judas Iscariot, Simon's son, who would betray Him, said, "Why was this fragrant oil not sold for three hundred denarii and given to the poor?" This he said, not that he cared for the poor, but because he was a thief, and had the money box; and he used to take what was put in it. But J-SUS said, "Let her alone; she has kept this for the day of My burial. For the poor you have with you always, but Me you do not have always." (John 12:3–8 – NKJV)

The world is not always going to understand your worship to the L-RD. It will even offend people who are not walking with G-D in intimacy. But worship Him anyway! It's not about who else is in the room, all that matters is that you're with the King. So keep your eyes on Him, quiet the noise around you, and pour out that extravagant love and worship to Him, no matter what the cost! And as sure as you pour out your love to Him, He is *so* good to pour back into you more than you would have ever thought possible!

Not by works of righteousness which we have done, but according to His mercy He saved us, through the washing of regeneration and renewing of the Holy Spirit, whom He poured out on us abundantly through J-SUS CHR-ST our Savior, (Titus 3:5–6 – NKJV)

Cleanse my lips, Lord,
wash away what is
impure; Let my
words be your words;
Let me be a
speaker of life
and truth.

Psalm 34:13 — Keep [my]
tongue from evil
and [my] lips from
speaking deceit.

"Cleanse my lips, L-RD, wash away what is impure. Let my words be Your words, let me be a speaker of *life* and truth."

Keep your tongue from evil, and your lips from speaking deceit. (Psalm 34:13 – ESV)

Gossip. That's an ugly word, we don't like to say that do we? It's easy to think that we're not speaking evil when we feel like, for the most part, we're not saying "bad" things. But what about those things that we're saying about a family member or a co-worker when they're not around? It may not be putting them down directly; sometimes we can tend to talk about others with the cover of, "I'm so worried about so and so because they are doing this, this, and this." The truth is, if we're spilling the beans about someone else's life without their permission, or without a pure motive of interceding on their behalf, then that's gossiping. When we just want something to talk about and a person comes to mind who's going through some hard things, or doing some things they shouldn't be doing and we start telling others all about it, that's gossiping, and that's some evil we just let slip onto our tongues. It's not the nicest thought, is it? But as we keep reading in that same chapter, G-D reminds us that He "redeems the soul of His servants, and none of those who trust in Him shall be condemned".

So if this is you, know that G-D is our redeemer, and the Blood of J-SUS was spilled to wash us clean and save us from *every* sin. There's nothing too dirty that He can't wash away. No wound too deep that He can't heal, because the truth is, sometimes words have created some of our deepest wounds. Maybe you were the one other people were gossiping about and it wounded your heart. Just turn to your Father G-D and trust in Him. Give Him your words; give Him the words that others have spoken about you, and *trust* that He has life to speak *through* you, as well as over you.

"She opens her mouth with wisdom, and the teaching of kindness is on her tongue." (Proverbs 31:26 – ESV)

As the deer pants for the water brooks, so pants my soul for You, O G-D. (Psalm 42:1 – NASV)

But those who wait on the L-RD shall renew their strength; they shall mount up with wings like eagles, They shall run and not be weary, They shall walk and not faint. (Isaiah 40:31 – ESV)

Faint has many different definitions. Besides the obvious of losing consciousness, losing physical strength, being weak or feeble, weak as in a color that is not bright, weak as in a sound that is not loud; it also means: cowardly, timorous, dejected, depressed, dispirited.

Maybe a couple of those words hit home with you as you read them. Things you're going through have you feeling weak, faint of heart, depressed, like you've lost your hope and can't seem to find the horizon; remember that there can still be peace in the midst of the storm. There is still hope. There is a promise to renew your strength and mount you up with wings like eagles! Your Father is not a G-D who makes promises He can't keep. What He says He will do you can *know* that it will be done! So find a quiet place to rest in His presence and let Him renew your spirit. Just get alone with your heavenly Father, tell Him your needs, your fears, your doubts, your troubles, your worries; there is nothing you can't tell Him. There is nothing you can say that will surprise Him. He already knows your heart, so pour it out to Him! And He will pour His goodness, peace, and comfort back into you.

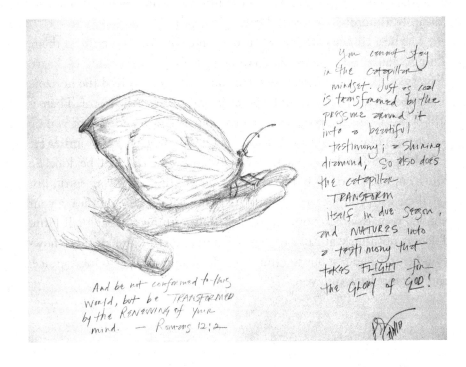

And be not conformed to this world, but be TRANSFORMED by the RENEWING of your mind. — Romans 12:2

You cannot stay in the caterpillar mindset. Just as coal is transformed by the pressure around it into a beautiful testimony; a shining diamond, so also does the caterpillar TRANSFORM itself in due season, and MATURES into a testimony that takes FLIGHT for the GLORY of GOD!

You cannot stay in the "caterpillar mindset". A dark, hard coal is transformed by the pressure around it into a beautiful testimony – a shining diamond. So also does the caterpillar *transform* itself in due season. It *matures* into a testimony that takes *flight* for the Glory of G-D!

So step up! And step *in* to the presence of G-D. He knows what He's doing with you, and when you submit to G-D and let the plans He has for you begin to unfold and take shape, the results are *beautiful!*

And do not ne conformed to this world, but be *transformed* by the renewing of your mind, that you may prove what is that good and acceptable and perfect will of G-D. (Romans 12:2 – NKJV)

Just as I parted the
Red Sea for moses,
So Shall I do for you.

"Just as I parted the Red Sea for Moses, so shall I do for you." – G-D

Then Moses stretched out his hand over the sea; and the L-RD caused the sea to go *back* by a strong east wind all that night, and made the sea into dry *land*, and the waters were divided. So the children of Israel went into the midst of the sea on the dry *ground*, and the waters were a wall to them on their right hand and on their left. And the Egyptians pursued and went after them into the midst of the sea, all Pharaoh's horses, his chariots, and his horsemen. Now it came to pass, in the morning watch, that the L-RD looked down upon the army of the Egyptians through the pillar of fire and cloud, and He troubled the army of the Egyptians. And He took off their chariot wheels, so that they drove them with difficulty; and the Egyptians said, "Let us flee from the face of Israel, for the L-RD fights for them against the Egyptians." (Exodus 14:21–25 – NKJV)

Don't forget who fights for you! Your Father is the G-D who parts the seas! He is the G-D of impossible things, and *He* fights for *you*! Nothing you face will ever be too big for Him to handle. *Trust* in the L-RD. Trust in the one who created the world and all of the great, incredible things in it, and still said we needed *you*.

I will raise my eyes to the mountains; from where does my help come from? My help comes from the L-RD, Who made heaven and earth. (Psalm 121:1–2 – NASV)

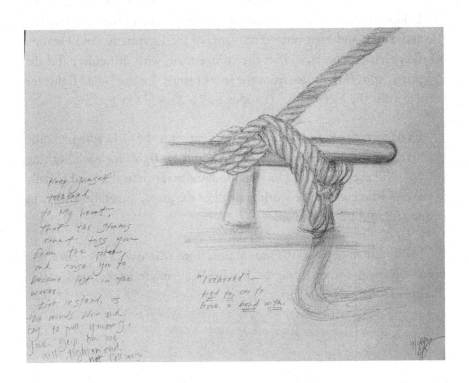

Tethered:
Tied to, or to have a *bond with*

"Keep yourself *tethered* to My heart, that the storms cannot toss you from the pier and cause you to become lost in the waves. But instead, as the winds blow and try to pull you away, your grip on Me will *tighten* and not fall away." – G-D

The L-RD is my strength and my shield; My heart trusts in Him, and *I am* helped; Therefore my heart triumphs, and with my song I shall thank Him. (*emphasis added*) (Psalm 28:7 – NASV)

Draw near to G-D and He will draw near to you. Cleanse your hands, you sinners; and purify your hearts you double-minded." (James 4:8 – ESV)

G-D has the ability. You have to be willing to *allow* Him to chisel away the hardness of your heart, and brush away the rubble, and bring out of that darkness a Child of G-D.

For you are all sons of G-D through faith in CHR-ST J-SUS. (Galatians 3:26 – NKJV)

Therefore you are no longer a slave, but a son; and if a son, then an heir through G-D. (Galatians 4:7 – NASV)

But as many as received Him, to them He gave the right to become children of G-D, to those who believe His Name, (John 1:12 – NKJV)

The enemy's main objective is to keep you from seeing your identity in G-D, because if you see and *know* who you are in Him, you are unstoppable. You are sons and daughters of the Most High G-D! You are His *beloved*. He's not an earthly parent who will disappoint you or abandon you, He is a *good* daddy who loves you more than you can imagine. He knows how many strands of hair are on your head, and not only has He seen and counted your tears, He keeps them saved in a bottle and has recorded *each* one! (Psalm 56:8) You matter to Him. You are seen by Him.

The enemy wants to keep you hardened by the ones who have let you down; he wants to keep your heart like stone so that it's too hard to feel the soft, gentle touch of G-D. Someone who has a hard heart will find it hard to believe G-D's love. A hard heart needs healing that can only come by the Blood of J-SUS. J-SUS was wounded, beaten, rejected, betrayed by His loved ones, insulted, cursed and abused; He suffered mercilessly, for you. So that you could be healed of your wounds. So that He could touch your heart in those deepest, darkest, hardest places, and heal and soften them. He bore the sins of *everyone* on earth, even the most vile that you can think of, He took those on upon Himself when He died for us on the cross. He took *your* sins, because He *loves* you, and *so greatly* wants you to know that love, and receive it, and walk in freedom, deliverance, healing, and that Shalom peace that surpasses understanding that comes from *knowing* you belong to G-D.

G-D's touch can penetrate deep down and pierce the hardness of heart.

His Word can reach down into those cold, stony places and pull out the treasure. We just have to let Him. Put your defenses down, and open your heart to His love for you, because He so deeply and truly does love you.

"Is not My Word like fire," declares the L-RD, "and like a hammer which shatters a rock?" (Jeremiah 23:29 – NASV)

A new heart also will I give you, and a new spirit will I put within you: and I will take away the stony heart out of your flesh, and I will give you an heart of flesh. (Ezekiel 36:26 – KJV)

For I am persuaded that neither death nor life, nor angels nor principalities nor powers, nor things present nor things to come, nor height nor depth, nor any other created thing, shall be able to separate us from the love of G-D which is in CHR-ST J-SUS our L-RD. (Romans 8:38–39 – NKJV)

But G-D demonstrates His own love for us in this: While we were still sinners, CHR-ST died for us. (Romans 5:8 – NIV)

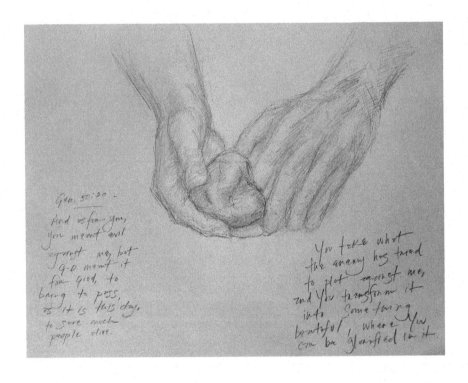

The word which came to Jeremiah from the L-RD, saying: "Arise and go down to the potter's house, and there I will cause you to hear My words." Then I went down to the potter's house, and there he was, making something on the wheel. And the vessel that he made of clay was marred in the hand of the potter; so he made it again into another vessel, as it seemed good to the potter to make. Then the word of the L-RD came to me, saying: "O house of Israel, can I not do with you as this potter?" says the L-RD. "Look, as the clay is in the potter's hand, so are you in My Hand, O house of Israel!" (Jeremiah 18:1–6 – NKJV)

And as for you, ye meant evil against me, but G-D meant it for good, to bring to pass, as it is this day, to save much people alive. (Genesis 50:20 – ASV)

L-RD, You take what the enemy has tried to plot against me, and You transform it into something beautiful where You can be glorified.

Just as the potter was able to take a seemingly ruined piece of pottery and reshape it, remold it, in his hands, transforming it into something better, so can G-D also do exactly that for you! In your life, in your marriage, in your children, in your family, in your finances, in your health, and in your mind; wherever you need transformation to take place, G-D is able! Trust the Potter, and put your circumstances in His Hands.

"If you would see yourself through *My* eyes, you would see just how much you *are* worthy. For the Blood of J-SUS covers you, and My love for you abounds." – G-D

You, dear children, are from G-D and have overcome them, because the one who is in you is greater than the one who is in the world. (1 John 4:4 – NIV)

You did not choose Me, but I chose you and appointed you that you should go and bear fruit, and that your fruit should remain, that whatever you ask the Father in My Name He may give you. (John 15:16 – NKJV)

,being confident of this very thing, that He who has begun a good work in you will complete it until the day of J-SUS CHR-ST; (Philippians 1:6 – NKJV)

Fear, doubt, insecurities – these are just a few things that fog up the mirror when we look at ourselves through our own eyes. We tend to see everything that's "wrong" with us first, and then we dwell on those things and end up beating ourselves down as we come up with all these reasons why we're not good enough. We are our own worst critics, and our own worst enemy. All of those harsh things we say about ourselves, G-D has *never*, and will never, say any of those things about us. He has never had even a bad *thought* about us, much less spoken a bad word concerning us. We are truly His beloved!

When the enemy tries to lie to you and say are "no good", G-D says "you are great!" When the enemy says you are unlovable, G-D says "you are My beloved! And My love for you is never ending"; when the enemy says you are worthless, G-D says "you are My greatest treasure. I have paid the highest price *just* for you, and I would do it all over again because you were worth *every* penny!"

Pray for each other. Do not forget to pray! Do not forget to intercede for one another that the people of G-D do not burn out and grow weary in their battles, or in their own prayer lives. Lift each other up. Always, always, always!

But Moses' hands became heavy; so they took a stone and put it under him, and he sat on it. And Aaron and Hur supported his hands, one on one side, and the other on the other side; and his hands were steady until the going down of the sun. So Joshua defeated Amalek and his people with the edge of the sword. (Exodus 17:12–13 – NKJV)

First of all, then, I urge that supplications, prayers, intercessions, and thanksgivings be made for all people. (1 Timothy 2:1 – ESV)

Praying at all times in the Spirit, with all prayer and supplication. To that end keep alert with all perseverance, making supplication for all the saints. (Ephesians 6:18 – ESV)

Not everyone belongs in your circle. Not everyone needs to know your business. But it *is* important to have a tight circle of people you trust, even if it's just one person that you can go to when you are in need of prayer. Otherwise we will get weary in the battle. It doesn't mean that we're not fighting the good fight and giving it our all. We are humans *designed* for connection. When G-D created Adam, He said it was not good for man to be alone, and created him a help-mate, his wife, Eve (Genesis 2:18). Everyone needs help at times during battle. Make sure that you remember to reach out when you are in need. And don't forget to be an Aaron and a Hur to others! When you see or know that someone else is fighting, battle *with* them! Intercede on their behalf. Pray for them. Strengthen your brother or sister. Pray for them, pray for your friends, pray for your loved ones, pray for your pastors, pray for the worship team, pray for those serving and those in leadership, and be the hand that holds up their arms when they are growing weary, so they can continue to push through and see the battle to the victory!

When you look at the definitions of "bear", here is what is you will see:

1. Carry the weight of; support.
2. Endure (an ordeal or difficulty)
3. (of a person) carry (someone or something)
   a. Be called by (a name or a title)
   b. Carry or conduct oneself in a particular manner
      i. "she bore herself with dignity"
4. Give birth to (a child)
5. Turn and proceed in a specified direction.
   a. "bear left and follow the old road"

You know that your father and his men; they are mighty warriors. Right now they are as enraged as a mother bear who has been robbed of her cubs. And remember that your father is an experienced man of war. He won't be spending the night among the troops. (2 Samuel 17:8 – NLT)

When the Bible mentions bears, it speaks of their ferocity, especially the fierceness when a mother bear is protecting her cubs or has them stolen from her. You don't mess with a momma bear's babies or you will most certainly catch her wrath! That's how we need to be when we're facing warfare and troublesome times. We aren't called to be timid; we're called to be **bold**! Sure and strong in the L-RD! Don't walk on the battlefield afraid to even look the enemy in his eyes, stand up strong against those trials, toss off the weight of what you're bearing and hand it over onto the shoulders of J-SUS, let a new strength be birthed forth in you, and step onto that battlefield like a raging bear protecting what belongs to you! Protecting the things that G-D has promised you, protecting your children and their generations, protecting your marriage, protecting and taking back what the enemy tried to steal from you! And when the enemy sees that Momma and Papa bear come barreling down the battlefield, charging him down head-on, he will *drop* what he thought he could take from you and *run*!

Be strong and courageous. Do not be afraid or terrified because of them, for the L-RD your G-D goes with you; He will never leave you nor forsake you. (Deuteronomy 31:6 – NIV)

You dont have to stay buried in the darkness; rise up on the wings of His Spirit and be lifted up, into His presence, out of the darkness, out of the pit.

You don't have to stay buried in the darkness; Rise up on the wings of His Spirit and be lifted up, into His presence, out of the darkness and out of the pit.

I waited patiently for the L-RD; He turned to me and heard my cry. He lifted me out of the slimy pit, out of the mud and mire; He set my feet on a rock and gave me a firm place to stand. He put a new song in my mouth, a hymn of praise to our G-D. Many will see and fear the L-RD and put their trust in Him. Blessed is the one who trusts in the L-RD, who does not look to the proud, to those who turn aside to false gods. Many, L-RD my G-D, are the wonders You have done, the things You planned for us. None one can compare with You; were I to speak and tell of Your deeds, they would be too many to declare. Sacrifice and offering You did not desire, but my ears You have opened; burnt offerings and sin offerings You did not require. (Psalm 40:1–6 – NIV)

G-D doesn't require anything from us in order to come before Him. He just wants *us*. You don't have to clean off the mud first before He will take you out of the pit, you just have to call out to Him. Let His Word pierce the ears of your heart and just cry out, "Yes, L-RD! I need *You*! Take me and do what You will!" and He will come to you right in the middle of your mess, and lift you up in Him. You may have dug your hole deeper than you think anyone can reach, but G-D is not afraid of the dark. He wants to pull you up into His light and cleanse you with the perfect Blood of J-SUS. If you let Him, He is good to take care of the rest.

He brought them out of darkness and the shadow of death, and broke their bands apart. (Psalm 107:14 – NASV)

For He rescued us from the domain of darkness, and transferred us to the kingdom of His beloved Son, in whom we have redemption, the forgiveness of sins. (Colossians 1:13–14 – NASV)

L-RD, bring me deeper into Your Holy Spirit, that my eyes may see through Your eyes, and see beneath the surface of what's around me, to the treasure.

A lot of times it's hard to see the bigger picture. We have so many distractions every single day. It's easy to get overwhelmed, and easy to get sidetracked. We see the crashing waves of the storm, we see all the things we need that we don't have at the moment, but G-D wants us to look through His eyes. Put on some Holy Spirit glasses and look what's beneath the surface; there is calmness and a peace when we step into a holy atmosphere, and there, we will see that provision has already been made for us.

The L-RD is not slow to fulfill His promise as some count slowness, but is patient toward you, not wishing that any should perish, but that all should reach repentance. (2 Peter 3:9 – ESV)

He is patient toward *you*. Did you catch that part? In those moments when we think He's just taking His sweet time, He's the one who is actually being patient towards *us*. He's waiting on us to get to that position in Him where we can handle the blessing and be good stewards of what it is He wants to give us; in the moment where it will have the biggest and best impact on our lives. Trust that He is a good Father, and He wants to give you your blessing even more than you want to receive it! Walk in obedience and faith, trust Him, listen to Him and act as the Holy Spirit leads you; set your eyes on the things of G-D, and know your needs will be met as you do these things.

But seek first the kingdom of G-D and His righteousness, and all these things will be added to you. (Matthew 6:33 – ESV)

When you feel like you have
been waiting so long, Remember:
G-D PREPARED HIS SON to be a
perfect sacrifice for us. He
was here PREPARING the way
for us. He IS PREPARING a
place for us.
Don't be
discouraged by
a wait, know
that your answer,
your place,
is being prepared.

Exodus 23:20
John 14:2-3
Mark 10:40
1 Cor. 2:9

You don't eat
when the food is
raw, you must
prepare, you must
wait for the oven
to heat to the right
temperature, wait for
the cook to be right, then eat.

You don't eat when the food is raw, you must first prepare, then you must wait for the oven to heat to the right temperature, wait for the cook to be right, and then eat well!

When you feel like you have been waiting so long, remember: G-D *prepared* His Son to be a perfect sacrifice for us. He was here *preparing* the way for us. He is *preparing* a place for us! Don't be discouraged by the wait. Know that your answer, your place, is being prepared.

Behold, I send an Angel before you to keep you in the way and to bring you into the place which I have prepared. (Exodus 23:20 – NKJV)

"Let not your heart be troubled; you believe in G-D, believe also in Me. In My Father's house are many mansions; if it were not so, I would have told you. I go to prepare a place for you. And if I go and prepare a place for you, I will come again and receive you to Myself; that where I am, there you may be also. (John 14:1–3 – NKJV)

But as it is written: "Eye has not seen, nor ear heard, Nor have entered into the heart of man the things which G-D has prepared for those who love Him. (1 Corinthians 2:9 – NKJV)

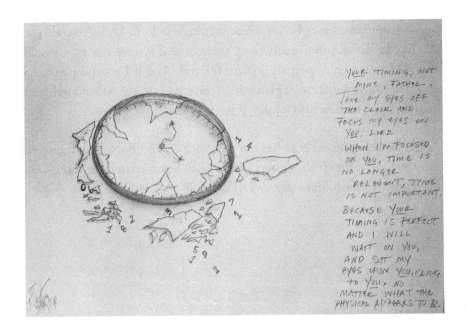

Your timing, Father, not mine.

Take my eyes off of the clock and focus my eyes on You, L-RD. When I'm focused on You, time is no longer relevant. Time is not important. Because Your timing is perfect, I will wait on You and set my eyes upon you; I will cling to You. No matter what the physical appears to be.

The L-RD is good to those whose hope is in Him, to the one who seeks Him; it is good to wait quietly for the salvation of the L-RD. (Lamentations 3:25–26 – NIV)

Wait quietly. How hard is *that* one? We kind of hate to even think about that, let alone say it out loud, don't we? No one likes waiting, especially when there's something that we need or want in the destination. That's why we're running, running, running! Hurry, hurry, hurry! Kids, you can brush your teeth and put your shoes on in the truck, we need to be on the road ten minutes ago! Eagle-eying as far down the road to try and watch out for state troopers so we can slow down before we get pulled over for speeding… those are just examples, of course, not something I actually do… You get what I'm talking about, though. We get in such a hurry so often, we find it hard to get out of that fast paced, has-to-be-now mentality, and we don't know how to slow down and just wait patiently when G-D is telling us, "Hold on. Not just yet". That's where the anxiety kicks in, and before we know it, we're bouncing our legs up and down, chewing on our fingernails, and making sure all the clocks are still working because things aren't happening on *our* time.

Quiet your soul. Wait patiently. Trust that G-D is moving, and He is working. Don't get so worked up about things that are *already* done! If G-D has already told you yes about things, *trust* Him! And patiently wait on the L-RD. He's got this.

A king does not worry what tomorrow will bring.

Stand strong and steady. There is peace in the L-RD. There is peace found in the knowledge of who you are, and *whose* you are. You belong to the Alpha and Omega, the King of kings. You are His.

What makes a king is not the clothes or the jewels or the crown. Those are simply things that are *placed* on the king. What *makes* a king is his behavior, his character; how he holds himself. A good king stands in strength and sureness in his authority. He doesn't need anyone to tell him what he is able to do, because he *knows* who he is, and what is his. A good king is alert and wise, careful with his words because he knows that each word he speaks is heard, weighed, and measured; he understands the influence his words carry. He is strategic and planned in all his ways so that he is not caught off guard by his foes. He cares for his people, and leads them in ways accordingly, because he knows that he is responsible for his kingdom. You are not called to be paupers; you are called to be kings and priests, so act like it!

And has made us kings and priests to His G-D and Father, to Him be glory and dominion forever and ever. Amen. (Revelation 1:6 – NKJV)

Keep the charge of the L-RD your G-D, to walk in His ways, to keep His statutes, His commandments, His ordinances, and His testimonies, according to what is written in the Law of Moses, that you may succeed in all that you do and wherever you turn. (1 Kings 2:3 – NASB 1995)

But you are a chosen generation, a royal priesthood, a holy nation, His own special people, that you may proclaim the praises of Him who called you out of darkness into His marvelous light; (1 Peter 2:9 – NKJV)

All it takes is a little faith to move mountains; all it takes is a little light to pierce the darkness.

When worries come, I will trust in You. When fear tries to overtake me, I will trust in You. Yours is the Hand that guides me when I can't see, Yours are the eyes that see the beginning and the end when I'm stumbling in the dark. When I let you take control, I don't have to be afraid of where my next step will be, because I know that when I keep my hand in Yours and let You lead, my feet will stay on the right path, and that path leads to every victory in You!

The L-RD Himself goes before you and will be with you; He will never leave you nor forsake you. Do not be afraid; do not be discouraged. (Deuteronomy 31:8 – NIV)

Direct my footsteps according to Your word; let no sin rule over me. (Psalm 119:133 – NIV)

When J-SUS spoke again to the people, He said, "I am the light of the world. Whoever follows Me will never walk in darkness, but will have the light of life." (John 8:12 – NIV)

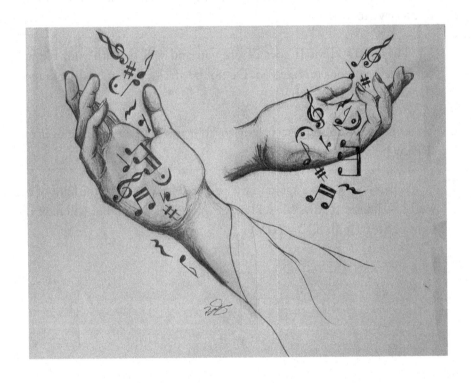

Because Your love is better than life, my lips will glorify You. I will praise You as long as I live, and in Your Name I will lift up my hands. (Psalm 63:3–4 – NIV)

Let everything that has breath praise the L-RD. Praise the L-RD! (Psalm 150:6 – NIV)

Let the message of Chr-st dwell among you richly as you teach and admonish one another with all wisdom though psalms, hymns, and songs from the Spirit, singing to G-D with gratitude in your hearts. (Colossians 3:16 – NIV)

There is power in your praise! There is testimony in your praise. When we're going through trials and hardships, it's easy to let the enemy steal our praise. We're so weary sometimes from life and the battles we're facing, that all we really want to do is curl up under some blankets and sleep until it's all over. The very last thing we want to do is sing songs of praise. But that's exactly where the enemy wants you. So heavy that even moving feels like you're doing it under the weight of the world. If you can let something out, though, anything at all, and start giving G-D your worship amidst your circumstances, He is *so* good to fill you with renewed strength. He will lift up that weight from you and strengthen you, and even if it still takes a little while for your circumstances to change in the natural, *know* that your worship is causing a shift in the spiritual. Just as Paul says in Ephesians 6:12-13 (NKJV) –

For we do not wrestle against flesh and blood, but against principalities, against powers, against the rulers of darkness of this age, against spiritual hosts of wickedness in the heavenly places. Therefore take up the whole armor of G-D, that you may be able to withstand in the evil day, and having done all, to stand.

So worship in those moments of darkness, worship in those moments of pain, worship despite the tears, worship until the atmosphere shifts and the light breaks in! For the weeping is but for a night, joy is coming in the morning! (Psalm 30:5)

Don't quit before the work is done! He is molding you in His Hands and smoothing out the surfaces. Allow the work to be done. Don't keep yourself a lump of clay on the potter's wheel.

But J-SUS answered them, "My Father has been working until now [He has never ceased working], and I too am working." (John 5:17 – Amplified Bible)

When we look at all the houses in our neighborhood, or the skyscrapers in the big cities, we rarely think about the process that went into building them. Drawing up the blueprints, proofing them and making sure the plans are all laid out without any potential problems down the line, preparing the plumbing, laying the foundations, putting up support beams and frames, wiring, insulation, windows, doors, roofing, siding, walling everything up, putting up ceilings. Once all the "hard" work is done, then it's time to make everything look nice, tidy, and appealing. Painting, laying floors, finding the right fixtures and furniture, all the nice little decorations that make everything pull together and feel homey and inviting; the character of the home or building begins to show up and shine.

We don't see that part when we're visiting friends or going into these big businesses, though. We just see the beautiful home they have made and live in with their families, or we admire the ornate décor the buildings adorn their walls with. The truth is, all of these things we admire and desire usually take a lot of hard work. Nothing is ever instant. We tend to forget that when we're waiting and praying for breakthrough in our lives or the lives of loved ones. Yes, there are times where there are instant miracles, but G-D's timing is perfect, and He knows exactly what we need and how much we can handle. If you feel a little impatient, just breathe, remember to trust your Creator, because He is always working. He doesn't take a lunch or go home for the day, He's *always* working, and working on our behalf. So don't give up before the project is completed! Because the outcome is going to be even more beautiful than you ever thought!

I step in. L-RD, focus me on You so that I do not fight against the current, but I flow in Your glory as Your current pulls me closer and further into Your presence. Saturate me, O L-RD.

He who believes in Me", as the scripture said, "From his inner most being will flow rivers of living water." (John 7:38 – NASB 1995)

And he showed me a pure river of water of life, clear as crystal, proceeding from the throne of G-D and of the Lamb. (Revelation 22:1 – NKJV)

LAMENTATIONS 3:23
GREAT IS HIS FAITHFULNESS;
HIS MERCIES BEGIN AFRESH
EACH MORNING.

ACTS 2:38 -39
EACH OF YOU MUST
REPENT OF YOUR SINS
AND TURN TO GOD, AND BE
BAPTIZED IN THE NAME OF
JESUS CHRIST FOR THE
FORGIVENESS OF YOUR SINS.
THEN YOU WILL RECEIVE THE
GIFT OF THE HOLY SPIRIT.
THIS PROMISE IS TO YOU, AND TO
YOUR CHILDREN, AND EVEN TO THE GENTILES —
ALL WHO HAVE BEEN CALLED BY THE LORD OUR GOD.

Great is His faithfulness, His mercies begin afresh each morning. (Lamentations 3:23 – NLT)

And Peter said to them, "Repent [change your old way of thinking, turn from your sinful ways, accept and follow J-SUS as the Messiah] and be baptized, each of you, in the Name of J-SUS CHR-ST because of the forgiveness of your sins; and you will receive the gift of the Holy Spirit. For the promise [of the Holy Spirit] is for you and your children and for all who are far away [including the Gentiles], as many as the L-RD our G-D calls to Himself." (Acts 2:38–39 – Amplified Bible)

That's a *promise* to you! I don't know about you, but that fills my heart with excitement! When G-D promises something He means it! And He keeps His promises! And that's all we have to do. Repent and turn to G-D.

Repentance is more than just saying you're sorry, it means changing your mind; to think differently afterwards. Repentance is turning away from what you were doing before, and doing things G-D's way from now on.

The sin of this world is enticing, yes. The devil would have an extremely hard time tempting any of us if sin didn't *look* good. But G-D also promises to always, always, always give us a way *out* of temptation. We don't *have* to fall into it! We do have a choice when those times come. We can choose to give in to flesh, or we can choose to rebuke those temptations and turn to G-D. G-D knew there would be times when we would fall, that's *why* He sent His Son to die for our sins. So we could always come back to our Father G-D, and when we truly repent, He has fresh mercy for us, ready to forgive and fill us with His presence. So don't think you've messed up "one too many times" or that G-D is just sick and tired of you by now. He isn't. His love for you is never ending!

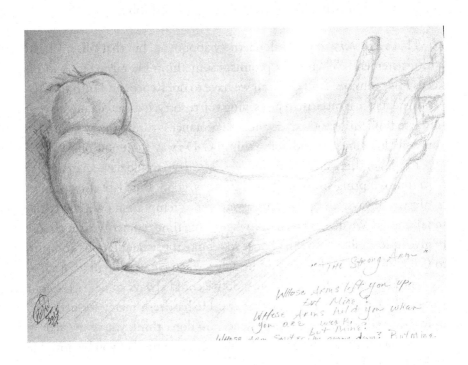

"The Strong Arm"

Whose Arms lift you up,
But Mine.
Whose Arms held you when
you are weak?
But Mine.
Whose arms Said... my arms down? But Mine.

"Whose arms lift you up, but Mine? Whose arms hold you when you are weak, but Mine? Whose arm smites the enemy down? But Mine." – G-D

For by their own sword they did not possess the land, and their own arm did not save them, But Your right hand and Your arm and the light of Your presence, For You favored them. (Psalm 44:3 – NASV)

Behold, the L-RD's Hand is not so short that it cannot save; Nor is His ear so dull that it cannot hear. (Isaiah 59:1 – NASV)

Who caused His glorious arm to go at the right hand of Moses, Who divided the waters before them to make for Himself an everlasting Name, (Isaiah 63:12 – ESV)

The strong right arm of the L-RD is raised in triumph. The strong right arm of the L-RD has done glorious things. (Psalm 118:16 – NLT)

The Eternal G-D is your refuge, and His everlasting arms are under you. He drives out the enemy before you. (Deuteronomy 33:27 – NLT)

He acted with a strong hand and powerful arm. His faithful love endures forever. (Psalm 136:11 – NLT)

It's impossible to imagine just how strong G-D's might really is. And yet even in His strength, He reaches out with such tenderness and love. He is our shield, our protector, and our provider, but also the lover of our hearts. He has the strength that sends the enemy running in fear, and that same strength He has He puts in us, too. Those strong arms that defeat armies and part the sea are also held open wide for you to run into His tender embrace.

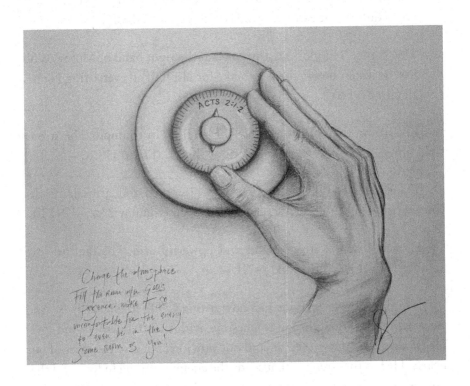

Change the atmosphere. Fill the room with G-D's presence; make it *so* uncomfortable for the enemy to even be in the same room as you!

When the Day of Pentecost had fully come, they were all with one accord in one place. And suddenly there came a sound from heaven, as of a rushing mighty wind, and it filled the whole house where they were sitting. (Acts 2:1–2 – NKJV)

It continues on in verses 3 and 4 (NKJV) – Then there appeared to them divided tongues, as of fire, and one sat upon each of them. And they were all filled with the Holy Spirit and began to speak with other tongues, as the Spirit gave them utterance.

The Holy Spirit changes the atmosphere we're in. When we're vigilant to consistently and constantly stay in a Holy Spirit atmosphere, we will be in a ready position to *respond* with the Holy Spirit rather than to *react* out of fleshly emotions like anger or offense. When stressful situations come up, we can respond in that peace that surpasses understanding, because we're standing in Holy Spirit atmosphere.

Down here in the south, it gets *hot*. We're talking eggs frying on the driveway, groceries that were frozen when you left the store are now completely thawed three blocks down the road while you're trying not to let your fingerprints get melted off from the steering wheel; changing clothes every time you come back in the house because you look like you fell in a swimming pool with all your clothes on after five minutes of being outside. It's hot! So you better believe our a/c is running and fans are blasting all through our nine months of summer! Point being, in absolutely *no way* do we want the atmosphere of our homes to match the atmosphere of what's outside our doors. Do you need to read that one more time? I'll wait. That crazy, hostile, toxic atmosphere of the world does *not* belong in your house. We need to be filled with the atmosphere of the Holy Spirit. We need to be so consumed by G-D's presence that the enemy can't handle it! And so filled with G-D that when we step into an atmosphere that is not of G-D, we can *immediately* recognize it, know exactly where that thermostat is, and change the atmosphere so that the whole house is filled with the presence of G-D!

"For your husband is your Maker, Whose name is the L-RD of armies; and your Redeemer is the Holy One of Israel, Who is called the G-D of all the earth. (Isaiah 54:5 – NASV)

"I will betroth you to Me forever, yes, I will betroth you to Me in righteousness and in justice, in lovingkindness and in compassion, and I will betroth you to Me in faithfulness. Then you will know the L-RD. (Hosea 2:19–20 – NASB 1995)

Let us rejoice and be glad and give the glory to Him, for the marriage of the Lamb has come and His bride has made herself ready." (Revelation 19:7 – NASB 1977)

"The kingdom of heaven may be compared to a king who gave a wedding feast for his son. (Matthew 22:2 – ESV)

In case you haven't noticed, G-D adores you! Yes, *you!* He is so passionately in love with you, but it's not like the earthly, oftentimes conditional, "love" that we've experienced from other people on this earth before. That is one of the things that make it so hard for us to comprehend not only the extent of G-D's love for us, but we find it hard to believe that He even likes us at all. When you've been constantly bashed, verbally or physically beaten down, or mistreated for any length of time, it's easier to see reasons why no one could possibly love you. When you don't even like yourself, it's hard to fathom someone loving you for you; someone loving you for who you are inside when you aren't even sure who you are. G-D knows who you are. You're His. You're His amazing, beautiful, specifically unique creation. He created you because He loved you even before you were made. He loved you *so* much He couldn't wait to create you! He put things inside of you that are so beautiful and strong, and the parts of you that the enemy tried to break, G-D wants to take those things, heal them, and make them *stronger*. Because there is shining glory in the strength that He's giving to you! And your story is not over, your time is not done, He's going to do great things with you, and you're going to know the right ways to show others how to give those broken pieces over to G-D and let Him mend and put them together in amazing ways!

"Sending out an atmosphere of praise"

G-D inhabits the praise of His people. So L-RD, I offer up my praise to You in every situation, that You may saturate my dwelling place and saturate those around me. Amen.

Indeed it came to pass, when the trumpeters and singers were as one, to make one sound to be heard in praising and thanking the L-RD, and when they lifted up their voice with the trumpets and cymbals and instruments of music, and praised the L-RD, saying: "For He is good, For His mercy endures forever," that the house, the house of the L-RD, was filled with a cloud, so that the priests could not continue ministering because of the cloud; for the glory of the L-RD filled the house of G-D. (2 Chronicles 5:13–14 – NKJV)

When we're in a place of worship, G-D begins to move! Worship Him with all of your heart! Let Him take over and stir up the room with his glorious presence!

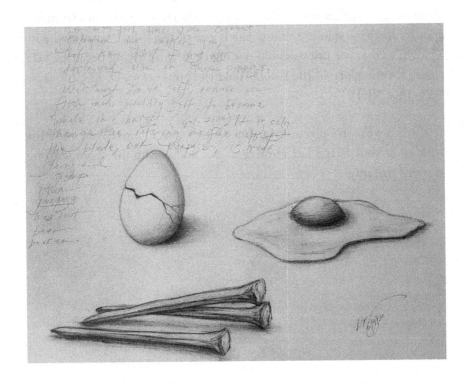

"If you want to make an omelet, you have to break some eggs." Everyone has heard that before. But never truer a saying. We often think about things breaking as being a bad thing, but when it comes to an eggshell, its entire existence is only complete once it has been broken. A chicken would never be if the chick didn't make that first break through the shell and into its first day of life on this earth. We would never have that wholesome breakfast or get that amazing cake made if we didn't crack that puppy open and obtain the contents for our purpose of both sustenance and pleasure. The fact of the matter is, the breaking does not mean you are broken. It's just part of the process of the bigger, better picture.

You may feel like your current situation has broken you, but know that it has *not* destroyed you or your purpose. We must die to self; remove our fleshly and worldly self, to become whole in Chr-st.

My old self has been crucified with Chr-st. It is no longer I who live, but Chr-st lives in me. So I live in this earthly body trusting in the Son of G-D, who loved me and gave Himself for me. (Galatians 2:20 – NLT)

It is only through the refining by fire that the blade, our purpose, is made strong and sharp. Your purpose has not been broken! You *are* coming out of this stronger, sharper, and shining!

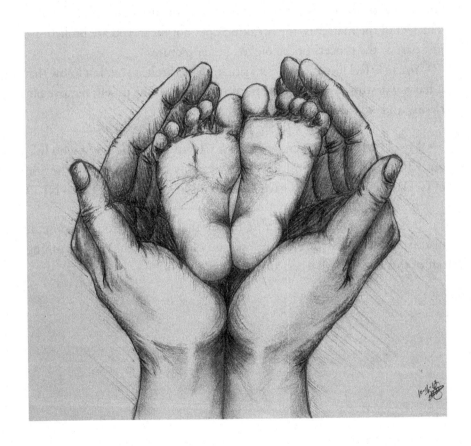

Blessed are those who mourn, for they will be comforted. (Matthew 5:4 – NIV)

The L-RD is close to the brokenhearted and saves those who are crushed in spirit. (Psalm 34:18 – NIV)

He heals the brokenhearted and binds up their wounds. (Psalm 147:3 – NIV)

This particular drawing was drawn in dedication to all those who have lost children; before or after they were able to be brought into this world. There are few words, if any, that can be offered to grieving parents. Our actions and words could never possibly be enough. If there is anyone who could understand that loss, though, it is G-D. And He is here to be your comfort and to hold you. These scriptures, and this drawing, are for you.

I love the L-RD, because He has heard My voice and my supplications. Because He has inclined His ear to me, therefore I will call upon Him as long as I live. The pains of death surrounded me, and the pangs of Sheol laid hold of me; I found trouble and sorrow. Then I called upon the Name of the L-RD: "O L-RD, I implore You, deliver my soul!" Gracious is the L-RD, and righteous; Yes, our G-D *is* merciful. The L-RD preserves the simple; I was brought low, and He saved me. Return to your rest, O my soul, for the L-RD has dealt bountifully with you. For You have delivered my soul from death, my eyes from tears, and my feet from falling. I will walk before the L-RD in the land of the living. (Psalm 116:1–9 – NKJV)

So you have an ugly past; G-D is in the business of taking something ugly, and turning it around into something beautiful for His glory.

So spread your wings! Feel His goodness and His glory rise you up higher. The ripples in the surface will calm in the stillness of His presence, and when you look at the reflection, look past what your earthly eyes see, and look at what He is showing you instead. You are His beautiful creation. The enemy may have tried to take you down early, and it felt like he was succeeding for a while, but G-D is saying, *My* child, you are *Mine!* Grow in Me and see what beauty you will be! For it's already been put inside of you! I planted it within you before you were even conceived! Where the enemy has tried to create crop failure, if you let Me, I will fertilize and water and feed you, and create an abundant harvest within you, and an even greater one with you!

But grow in the grace and knowledge of our L-RD and Savior J-SUS CHR-ST. To Him be the glory both now and forever. Amen. (2 Peter 3:18 –NKJV)

Blessed be the G-D and Father of our L-RD J-SUS CHR-ST, the Father of mercies and G-D of all comfort, who comforts us in all our tribulation, that we may be able to comfort those who are in any trouble, with the comfort with which we ourselves are comforted by G-D. For as the sufferings of Chr-st abound in us, so our consolation also abounds through Christ. (2 Corinthians 1:3–5 – NKJV)

He comforts us in all our troubles so that we can comfort others. When they are troubled, we will be able to give them the comfort G-D has given us.

There are certain people that you will be able to minister to that other people would have a hard time reaching, because you have cried the same tears, you have had the same fears, but you have the testimony of victory in G-D. You were pulled out of that same darkness and will be able to recognize it in someone struggling in the same way.

You hold the key to someone else walking out victorious! Do not hide your testimony. Do not put away those keys. Just as there was a purpose for the suffering of J-SUS, there is a purpose for what you went through, and it is to help others like you.

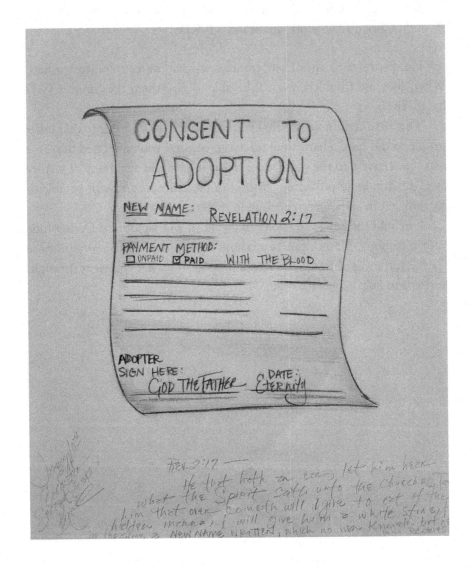

"He who has an ear, let him hear what the Spirit says to the churches. To him who overcomes I will give some of the hidden manna to eat. And I will give him a white stone, and on the stone a new name written which no one knows except him who receives it." (Revelation 2:17 – NKJV)

"He defends the cause of the fatherless and the widow, and loves the foreigner residing among you, giving them food and clothing." (Deuteronomy 10:18 – NIV)

"The King will reply, 'Truly I tell you, whatever you did for one of the least of these brothers and sisters of mine, you did for me." (Matthew 25:40 – NIV)

You don't have to feel alone in this world. You don't have to feel like you have been abandoned. You are not only immeasurably loved by your Father, He has adopted you into His kingdom. He said there is no price too great, there is no price He would not pay, for you. He longs for you. He longs for you to know the extent of His love. He paid the ultimate price and made the greatest sacrifice for you to know Him; for you to be able to come into His kingdom, into His family, because you matter *that much* to Him.

There is not a single tear you can cry that goes unnoticed. G-D not only sees each one, but He catches them all in the palm of His loving Hands.

What matters to you, matters to G-D. Your heart's cry is not in vain, nor is your pain invisible. Know that the tender embrace of your Father is holding you in the midst of it all. You are not alone, not now and not ever. You have a Father who is for you, even when it seems like the world is against you. Chin up, sons and daughters; lift your eyes up off the ground and look up towards your Father who is with you and for you always.

Blessed are those who mourn, for they *WILL* be comforted. (emphasis added) (Matthew 5:4 – NIV)

"You number my wanderings; Put my tears in Your bottle; are they not in Your book? When I cry out to You, Then my enemies will turn back; This I know, because G-D is for me. In G-D (I will praise His word), In the L-RD (I will praise His word), In G-D I have put my trust; I will not be afraid. What can man do to me? (Psalm 56:8–11 – NKJV)

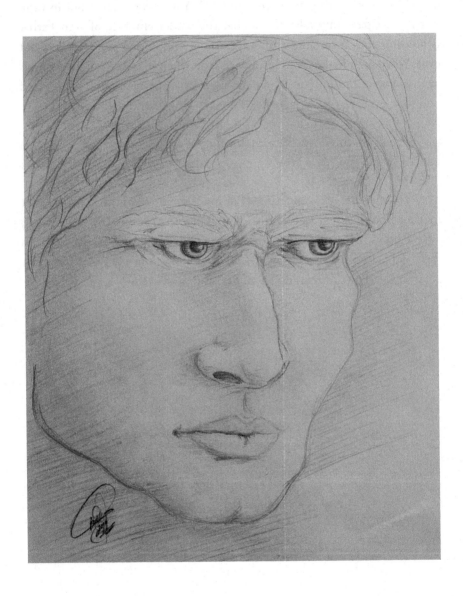

I will stand strong against the adversary! For G-D is my Father! I cry Y-hweh is His holy Name! My battle cry is fiercer than the enemy's for G-D is my strength; He is my shield. He is my protector and He has clothed me with His armor and put His sword in my hand! My Father is for me, *nothing* can be against me! I stand in the evil day, and withstand! Amen!

Therefore, take up the full armor of G-D, so that you will be able to resist on the evil day, and having done everything, to stand firm. (Ephesians 6:13 – NASB)

These things I have spoken to you, so that in Me you may have peace. In the world you have tribulation, but take courage; I have overcome the world." (John 16:33 – NASB 1995)

Have I not commanded you? Be strong and courageous! Do not tremble or be dismayed, for the L-RD your G-D is with you wherever you go." (Joshua 1:9 – NASB 1995)

I have fought the good fight, I have finished the race, I have kept the faith. Henceforth there is laid up for me the crown of righteousness, which the L-RD, the righteous judge, will award to me on that day, and not only me but also to all who have loved His appearing. (2 Timothy 4:7–8 – ESV)

You are mighty warriors and soldiers in a battle whose only outcome is victory! What is there to be afraid of? Don't lose heart. Don't let hopelessness seep in. Do not fear. You are on a battleground and those are the only weapons the enemy has in his arsenal. You carry the *true* weapons of warfare; you have the armor of G-D to put on! And all of heaven's angel armies are on your side!

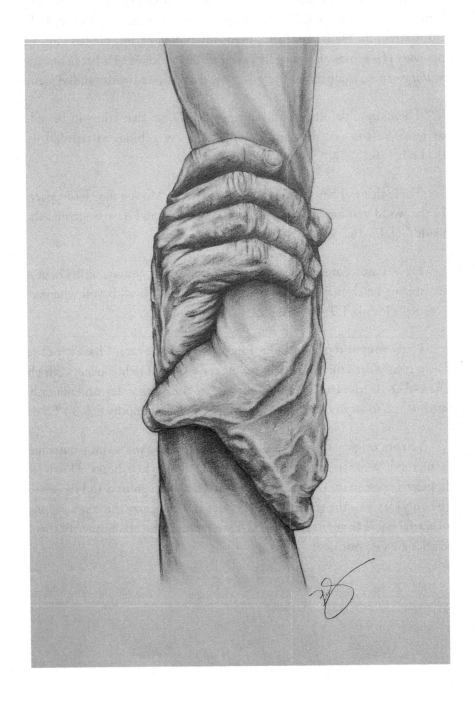

He brought me up out of the pit of destruction, out of the mud; and He set my feet on a rock, making my footsteps firm. (Psalm 40:2 – NASB)

This piece was drawn specifically for all those who are struggling with addiction, and all those who are walking in their recovery from addiction. Whether it is drugs, alcohol, pornography, lust, food, self harm – whatever addiction you're battling right now, you're never too deep for G-D to reach in and pull you out. He is *right there* with you. He sees you. And He's not there in anger, He's there as a Father who deeply, unconditionally loves His son, who unconditionally loves his daughter, and who is reaching for you, never letting His hand fall away. He is just waiting for you to say "Yes, L-RD" and take His hand so He can pull you up out of that pit of destruction.

Where can I go from Your Spirit? Or where can I flee from Your presence? If I ascend into heaven, You are there; If I make my bed in hell, behold, You are there. If I take the wings of the morning, and dwell in the uttermost parts of the sea, Even there Your Hand shall lead me. And Your right Hand shall hold me. If I say, "Surely the darkness shall fall on me," Even the night shall be light about me; Indeed, the darkness shall not hide from You, But the night shines as the day; The darkness and light are both alike to You. For You formed my inward parts; You covered me in my mother's womb. (Psalm 139:7–13 – NKJV)

How precious also are Your thoughts to me, O G-D! How great is the sum of them! If I should count them, they would be more in number than the sand; When I awake, I am still with You. (Psalm 139:17–18 – NKJV)

G-D not only sees you, but He also *knows* you. He knows your thoughts, and your innermost parts. And not only is He *with* you, but He *wants* you! And despite the pit you are in, He thinks *good* thoughts about you! So many that you cannot even count them. Stop listening to the lies of the devil. *Hear* the Words of the L-RD! *Listen* to what G-D is saying, and grab His hand that He has been reaching out to you this whole time. Put everything else aside and cling to your Father who loves you.

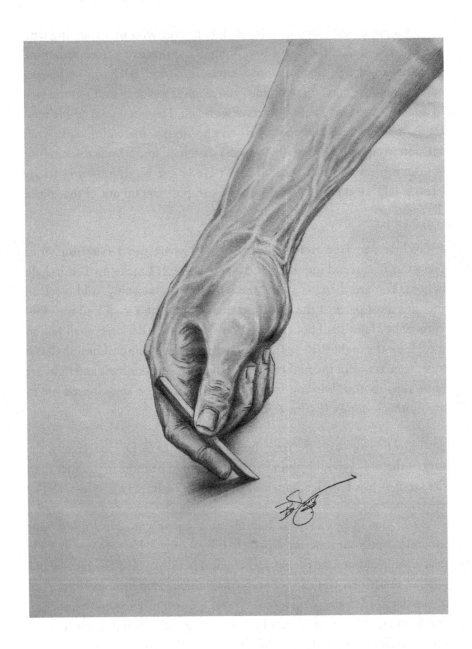

"For I know the plans I have for you," declares the L-RD, "plans to prosper you and not to harm you, plans to give you hope and a future." (Jeremiah 29:11 – NIV)

How many times have we tried to fulfill our own will in our lives? How many times has that ended in disaster? I can't count the times where I tried to take over and do things *my* way, thinking I knew better than my Father. I know what I need, I know what will make things work best, and I know when the timing should be… No. I don't. Each and every time I tried to take the reins you better believe it was an ugly crash. But G-D is so good, and every time I turned back to Him in repentance for not trusting His plans, and placed my situation back into His well-able hands, He has always been so good at turning what I thought was a fiery disaster of failure into a blazing glory of victory instead. When we trust *His* timing, when we seek *His* will for our lives, when we pursue *His* plans for us, that is when favor falls upon us and the way is made. Even when it looks like there is no way, He parts the sea and makes a way; because His plans for us are *good*. His plans for us are *hope*. And there *is* a future for you.

CHAPTER 3

So many times I've wanted to just shake people and scream in their faces, *"How do you not know how **loved** you are!? How can you not know!?"* It drives me crazy to see people who are struggling with feeling unloved; unloved by family members, unloved by their spouses, unloved by friends, unloved by seemingly everyone, and ultimately feeling unloved by G-D. They're so desperate for acceptance and they are yearning for someone to just *see* them and love them; they're reaching out to whoever is within their grasp to get it. The problem with that is, they will usually hold onto the first person their fingers touch. *People* are not perfect, and they will so often disappoint you. That's why G-D says not to put our faith in the people of this world, which are temporary, but to put our trust and faith in Him (Psalm 146:2–4). Our fulfillment comes from our Father G-D, not from the things of this world. That hole that you're trying to fill is G-D shaped, that's why nothing else will fit. The pain that you're trying to mask and hide doesn't need to be buried deep down, it needs to be lifted up and given away to Abba Father.

You are so deeply, greatly loved and cherished. You think you're unworthy, and the truth is, we are *all* unworthy. That's the whole point! J-sus died on the cross and shed His Blood to be the perfect sacrifice that *makes* you worthy! For His Blood covers a *multitude* of sins! (Col. 1:20; Eph. 1:7; Heb. 9:14, etc.) He did that for *you*. He did that out of *love* for you! Because He knew you would need Him; He knew you would have times of weakness, fear, and doubt and would need Him; He knew you would need His love, and He wanted to make sure that you had *access* to Him every second of every day of your life! Because it's not just about when we feel like we need Him, because, truthfully we *always* need Him, it's about a relationship with Him. And if you give your whole heart to Him, open up and truly be honest with Him, it's the most amazing relationship you could ever have!

Through intimacy with Him and knowing J-sus, you receive your identity in Him. You can confidently know who you are in Chr-st, because of who He calls you; you *are* His beloved.

My prayer for you in reading this book is for it to open your eyes to see through G-D's eyes. I pray it would help awaken your heart with a passionate love for your Father G-D. I pray that it would stir up the revelation of His passionate love for *you*. That you would *see* His love for you, feel His love for you, and that it would overflow from within you onto those around you. I pray that it would cause your relationship with Him to shift into something deeper; into what He meant for it to be.

If you've been feeling dry and weary, I pray and declare life over you, and that your spirit would arise in joy, strength, and renewed passion that is uncontainable. I pray that you would receive the unconditional love of the Father, and be a vessel to share it with those around you and speak into the lives of those in need.

Be blessed, bride of Chr-st, and *know* that you are so greatly, profoundly, and unconditionally *loved*.

Printed in the United States
by Baker & Taylor Publisher Services